I0135376

Missouri Poems

Missouri Poems
With a Touch of Wales

Jon Dressel

GREEN ALTAR BOOKS
SHOTWELL PUBLISHING

Missouri Poems With a Touch of Wales
Copyright© 2024 by Jon Dressel

ALL RIGHTS RESERVED. No part of this publication may be reproduced, distributed, or transmitted in any form or by any means, including photo-copying, recording, or other electronic or mechanical methods, or by any information storage and retrieval system without the prior written permis-sion of the publisher, except in the case of very brief quotations embodied in critical reviews and certain other non-commercial uses permitted by copyright law.

Published by GREEN ALTAR BOOKS,
an imprint of
SHOTWELL PUBLISHING LLC
Post Office Box 2592
Columbia, So. Carolina 29202
www.ShotwellPublishing.com

ISBN: 9978-1-963506-28-0

FIRST EDITION

10 9 8 7 6 5 4 3 2

Produced in the Republic of South Carolina

For Barbara Marshman Dressel,
valiant to the end.

The Last Taco, A Love Song

We were not in Paris but our kitchen,
where, as always, she had planned
the meal. We had a deal: I did
the work, while she, from her wheelchair,
lent advice. On that night
her tips were few. I had a simple
set of tasks. I got a skillet, browned
ground beef, stirring seasoned
powder in. I took the knife she judged
was best, cut up lettuce, sliced
an avocado. I got sour cream
and salsa from the fridge. Then,
not quite as she'd proposed, I clapped
the lot together on two brittle,
flat tortillas. She smiled amused
approval as I set the plate
before her. She ate only a bit
of hers, but we lingered
at the table for an hour and talked.
I rinsed the dishes, then we went to bed.
The cancer took her two nights on.

Acknowledgments

Some of these poems were first published in the following periodicals and anthologies:

Poetry Wales; The Anglo-Welsh Review; Planet; The New Welsh Review; Roundyhouse; Prairie Schooner; Kansas Quarterly; Counter/Measures; Chronicles; The Works (Welsh Union of Writers); *Prize Winners' Anthology*, Arvon Foundation International Poetry Competition, 1985; *Prize Winners Anthology, British National Poetry Competition* (The Poetry Society, London), 1989.

Several poems have also been broadcast on BBC-2.

Beethoven at the Alamo was broadcast, read by the author, on National Public Radio's *All Things Considered* on Beethoven's birthday (December 16), 1996.

Lot: Some Speculations received the First Award of Borestone Mountain Poetry Awards (Palo Alto,California) in 1976 as "The best poem published in a periodical in 1975 in the English-speaking world".

CONTENTS

THERE WAS A WAR

PRICE OF VIRGINIA: MISSOURI'S MAN

A TOUCH OF WALES

SEARCHING THE SCRIPTURES

THE PLACE WHERE TWO GREAT RIVERS MEET

WHERE DOES THE SOUTH BEGIN?

THE MAN WHO...

REMEMBERED

BEETHOVEN AT THE ALAMO
AND OTHER POEMS

Foreword

A Poet of Many Voices

by Catharine Savage Brosman

THE LATE JON DRESSEL, of St. Louis, whose career ended with his death in 2024, was a splendid poet with too little recognition. Although well known in Wales, an adoptive home, he was almost a poet without honor in his own country. Yet he studied at Northwestern University and Washington University, St. Louis, taught at Webster University, in that city, and later took a Ph.D. in American Studies at St. Louis University. In cooperation with the University of Central Iowa, he established a program for American students at Trinity College Carmarthen in Wales. He subsequently spent considerable time in that country, where fellow poets and readers may have discovered their sympathy for the American South and its history. His collection *The Road to Shiloh* appeared there, and he even composed part of his work in Welsh. Those facts may shed light on his low profile in America. In bringing out this new volume, the present publishers have rendered a significant service to American, particularly southern, letters.

Dressel was a poet not only of two languages but of many voices. He gives imaginative life to figures of the past and present, speaking singly or in concert with, or against, each other, across times, across an ocean. Above them all is the poet's own voice, as he invisibly muses or directs the dramas—a metafigure guessed at or heard, as when he addresses a character using the second person.

Additionally, Dressel was a master of technique— tone, beat, form and shaping of poems, including stanza and line length choices and rhyme when he wishes. (Beat is essential; as Donald Stanford observed, "Without rhythm, the poem is dead.") Dressel's lines move easily, making poems nearly as fluid as the mind itself. Blank verse, which he utilized to good effect, is a recurrent form; his free verse is often marked by quasi-iambic lines. "A Southern Soldier Answers Near the Year 2000" and "For the Dun Dove" are impressive villanelles.

Except for the initial poem, "The Last Taco," a homage to the poet's late wife, the collection is arranged in thematic clusters. Historical and contemporary scenes contrast with each other, rural with urban settings. Beginning with "In Memoriam: The Monument in the Park" and "The Man on the Horse," many poems are connected to the American South, from earliest Virginia through the war of 1861-1865 to the present. "Dawn Tide, Jamestown, 1611" features a Welshman named ab Rhys (changed to "Price"), one of the first American Welsh settlers. A descendant of his serves later as governor of Missouri (see "Price of Virginia, Missouri's Man").

The destructive war of the 1860s is central. In the two-part "Ghost Talk," one of numerous strong war poems, U.S. Grant and Albert Sidney Johnston, the

opposing commanders at Shiloh, meet in the pres-
ent time—a bold but effective act of the poet's imagi-
nation—and look back together to the battle some
150 years earlier. In tones of regret, each challenges
the other while entirely aware of how circumstances
trapped them. What is a righteous cause? Johnston
claims he was "defending what was all worth fighting
for"—homes, wives, way of life. If you // had broken
with us, and we had invaded Ohio, / you would have
felt the same." His old adversary counters by observ-
ing, "It was you, after all, that had the slaves." But,
thinking of the lost cause, the counter-factual south-
ern victory, Johnston retorts, "I doubt it could have
turned out worse for them. / We would have freed
them ourselves by the century's / end, might have got
by with less violence ...." He concludes, "You surely
know there are worse causes now."

Grant is an actor in "Corinth" and Johnston in "The
Landing." The poem entitled "From 'The Road to Shi-
loh'" is a lengthy lamentation with biblical echoes. In
"Central Missouri, 1864," a long war narrative, Ster-
ling Price reappears, paralleled roughly with Owain
Glyndwr (Owen Glendower) in a similar situation.

Among other poems associated with Welsh history
and contemporary Wales are "The Holy Well," "The
Elm Bush," illustrating man and nature together, and
the delightful "The Cockle Man." Other outstanding
poems include "The Pentacostal Duck," and "A Clutch
Conjunction," both with a Christian dimension. "A
Dog Gone" depicts canine excellence and human de-
votion to another species.

Dressel's mastery of idiom is evident in "The Man
Who Forgot He Ate His Lunch" (from a series "The Man
Who ..."). It portrays in what would be his own tones

and diction an old St. Louis saxophonist, playing in Gaslight Square, an authentic figure, man and music almost one. "The day he dropped that man blew jazz."

This welcome volume of selected writings offers an opportunity for the American literary public to appreciate Dressl's contributions. Southern readers and the librarians and booksellers who assist them should add it to their lists.

Jon Dressel:

A Memoir by His Son
Benjamin Marshman Dressel

ANGLO WELSH POET, editor and man of letters
Raymond Garlick was my father's dearest friend
and trusted literary confident. As a student in his
poetry class I once asked him how a poet might be
considered "great". His response was the poet should
have written at least 6 poems that were "world" class.
By this definition, he mused, Dylan Thomas might be
one short! I doubt my father would qualify by these
standards, but it must be said he was a fine poet and
penned several world class poems of his own, not
least of which was a series of poems judged to win the
"crown" at the national Eisteddfod in Wales in 1976.
The poems were written in English and translated
by T. James Jones into bardic Welsh. Although later
disqualified due to the "collaboration," it served as one
of his finest poetic achievement and a moment of great
personal satisfaction.

Jon Dressel began his writing career not as a poet
but a newspaper editor. Both in high school and later
as the editor of the *Daily Northwestern*. After serving
out his ROTC commitment at the Brooklyn Navy yard
he was set to attend Harvard to complete an MBA and

go on to a career as an editor, but his father's poor health forced him back to Granite City and the family dairy business. That experience left him with a sense that perhaps an MBA wasn't the path forward and he opted instead to pursue his interest in creative writing at Washington University. After completing an MFA he went on to teach literature and creative writing at Webster University in St. Louis.

It was during this period that he re-discovered his family's connection to Wales. Through trips and then living and working in Wales his true "self" as a writer would emerge. We moved to Wales as a family in 1976, not long after dad had won the prestigious Borestone Mountain Poetry Award for the best poem published in English in 1975, "Lot, Some Speculations". The tight "triplet" verses he composed in that, and other poems of that era were some of his finest efforts as a poet and found their way into publication frequently.

The years spent in Wales were, I'm sure, some of my father's happiest. His identity as an "Anglo Welsh" poet was well respected in the literary community in Wales although he was often referred to as the "Yank-lo" Welsh poet. His passion for Wales and exploring his Welsh heritage played out in the writing and led to many wonderful poems celebrating the life and characters of a small Welsh village. Life's twists and turns eventually led my father back to St. Louis where he opened his 2nd pub, an establishment dedicated to a celebration of the Arts and Literature. His interest in the Civil War inspired his writings from that time but Wales and the bardic tradition were always the grounding force that drove him.

I don't recall my father writing much of anything during my mother's 5-year battle with lung cancer.

Their time was spent alternating between the hospital and road tripping, making the most of the dying of the light. After her passing he wrote what must have been the most bitter-sweet of poems, "The Last Taco." He was known as Pop Pop in our house. On his penultimate night in hospital, he shared his thoughts on this collection of poems with my wife and there was no doubt that it had given his life purpose and joy to bring his final worldly legacy to the finish line.

He had run the family dairy for 7 long years before he "escaped" to find himself in the literary world. There was irony in his chuckle when he said goodbye to his grandson Pascal while finishing his hospital dessert. "Pop Pop sure loves ice cream." And so it was on his last day, he sipped a McDonald's milkshake with his devoted daughter Beth, the mix for which he had helped develop all those years ago at the dairy in Granite City.

He passed quietly in the morning, 4 days short of his 90th year, to heaven. We miss him.

There Was a War

In Memoriam:
The Monument in the Park

I

Laurel-crowned and massive on its plinth,
the stone had stood a century in the Park,
attended by a cordon of massive oaks.
Words of Lee and Davis were cut into
its granite, and in a bronze relief below,
a youth, face turned from elders at a door,
was shown departing, one presumed, for war.

II

Passers on a path nearby, of both
races, out for air, would sometimes stop,
approach the stone, take a turn, at ease,
around it, pausing to peruse the words,
observe the bronze, and then, their detour
    done,
walk on. It was as though they took
the stone to be intrinsic, of the Park.

III

Boy shot—police—pent anger flared, and then,
with guidance, sought for marks. Some held
    the stone
at heart involved, a mask for stark, primordial
wrong. Crowds were marshaled, stormed it
nightly, shouting that it must come
down. Power pondered, then complied,
sent the cranes and tractors in
to tug and growl until they had it gone,

IV

Men came with trucks, applied fresh sod.
Now, months on, the grass well spread,
one might pretend the stone was never there
except, at times, for passers on the path
who stop to stare, to contemplate the ground,
as though they sense an emptiness abides
amid webbed shadows of the towering trees.

♦

The Man on the Horse

Franz Sigel was his name. He had studied
war in Germany, fought in the risings of '48,
come to St. Louis when the risings failed,
joined the host of Teuton migrants here.
He became a colonel in the Union Army,
met with bleak defeat at Wilson's Creek.
A general later, shifted east, he was routed
at New Market in the Shenandoah,
never saw command again. He remained
a hero to German-America; when he died
in New York four decades on, thousands
marched in his funeral cortege.

He sits embronzed on his horse in the Park,
near where the Confederate monument stood.
He is hunched in his saddle, staring straight
    ahead,
a sculptor's model of a grim resolve,
in face, perhaps, of gray doom coming on.
No matter; time has changed and rendered him
triumphant, his monumental enemy
pulled down and hauled away. One wonders,
though, if bronze could speak, what he might say:
would he exult, or feel he had been wronged
to be thus stripped of nearness to the foe,
and left to joggers, dogs and passing cars?

♦

Notes from Wilson Creek
August 10, 2015

I

The lines of sight are not what they were then,
trees and brush and time have intervened
to skew, for us, the vision that men had

on these stubbed hills and stump-cleared fields
as this day broke in Eighteen Sixty-One
down in the left-hand corner of Missouri

where the Ozark highlands gently rise to south
and not far west, the bleeding Kansas plains
commence the long ascent towards rocked divide.

The lines are altered, not what they were then,
yet we still come, to see it as we can,
this day in shimmering August in a year

some fifteen tortuous decades down the road
from that charged summer when the fire back east
made leap a thousand miles, and hell blew here.

II

The modest lot for cars is nearly full,
rangers wave us to a vacant slot.
We partake of lemonade and oatmeal cookies

in the bustling lobby of the Visitors Center
where uniformed pretenders and their ladies
on bright gingham mingle unabashedly

with tourists less observant albatrossed
by cameras and more absently attired.
A live voice sounds, invites us to a room,

a slide show built on Bingham has its say,
we file out after, rim a contour map,
a tape intones, deployments of small lights

flash on, go dark do service as they can
to limn the battle in the mind's cold eye.
It ends; we occupy the bookshop's aisles

make both casual and more earnest buys,
and then, our time arrived, go out,
into the neutral glare of August noon.

III

The driving tour has kindred in Virginia,

Mississippi, Georgia, Tennessee,

numbered stops, where placards, like stern
    guardsmen,

stand attention with their terse, clean prose,

present as well, when clarity commands

it, reinforcing map and sketch, and sometimes

boast an adjunct box which, button pushed,

snaps to with sound. At one such we walk
    downward

from the road that wends its way, ordained,

around the field, descend through woods, and
    reach

the Creek. The shade is flecked with sun, yet cool.

The thirsting grass, above, has gone half-brown,

odd insects buzz in heat along baked paths

where no dust lies sufficient to raise cloud,

but here, the water ripples bright, then green,

beside the scant stone tracings of a mill

where Union soldiers, in the thin dawn light

picked their way through bankside bramble,
    found

a place to make a ford, splashed across
and then went up, entered on a spreading
cornfield, met with Southern concentration,

stopped and formed in line behind a rail-fence,
gave fire, got it, devil take the stalks,
were charged, forced back, near broken in retreat,

until, in nick of Yankee time, their distant cannon
shot those left the cover to go down,
back down through brush and bramble to the
    Creek,

to cross again, by here, by Gibson's Mill,
where on this day the shade is dappling cool
and water ripples bright, and then dark green.

IV

You, John Ray, stout man of Tennessee,
trek to deep Missouri as the forties wane,
bereft, one daughter, court and marry

the Widow Steele, four offspring of her own
(you and she will get six more, in time),
acquire the estate of your bride's late husband,

take possession of the modest farm,
title to Wiley and Rhoda as well, freight
of the property, their four children yours

too when they come. and lay hands on
to work the place, by which a branch meanders
that is known as Wilson Creek.

(Wilson, buckskin, came in with the Delawares, wed
three times to Indian women, chased each off,
thought upon Saint Louis, rode long, bid,

got there a French girl for a final wife
and backtracked quick to his hill-pitch here
where the James River takes on board a stream

that went by his name then, and will forever.)
You, John Ray, dig in, plank floor, hoist beam,
raise, well-angled to the winds, a dwelling,

sturdy, roofed porch fronting on the road
along which Morse-wrought wire will later string,
and down whose ruts the fertile country's load

of produce moves. You prosper, keep bees,
horses, dogs and cows, grow abundant grain
for market, get made postmaster, seize

ripe chance, become by right a local main-
man, the stage arrives before your door,
the folk call in, and times wax fat and good

until that potent August when the fire
bursts here, guns roar, lead rips the living wood
and you, John Ray, reluctant, harbor war.

V

John Ray, your house persists in time, restored,
the only structure present on the field
that eyes from then, returned to light, might know.

We park below it on a tarmac lot, climb stairs
incised into the hill to ease the tourist
foot's ascent, attain the top, the Wire Road's

trace, traverse the yard, mount steps again,
then cross the porch, glance back, go in.
We pause, alone. Word-sounds reach us from
    a room

beyond, we move on, mingle, nod and talk,
inspect arrayed utensils of that century
most our own, and cock our ears respectful

as a plain-clad volunteer explains
to us the workings of a country kitchen
instant on the virgin musket-crack,

and tells then how the house and yard
soon filled with Southern fighting men, with maimed
and dying, tenders to them, how shells burst near.

took out the coop, splinters, hen-parts, straw
and feathers flying, and how then, a yellow
flag displayed (no red cross yet), they

ceased to come. Shafts of sunlight streak the spare
front room, we view the bed, the counterpane,
on which unyielding Lyon's corpse (he who

would have seen Missouri dead and buried
had his cause of Union, sacred, so demanded),
left in last confusion by a tree as wagons

piled with men whose wounds were live
began to lumber northward in retreat,
had lain, with friends attendant, by the grace

of Sterling Price. We exit, stand in roof-shade
on the porch, as you did on that deafening
morning, you, John Ray, confronting August

sun, the fury in your neighbor's corn,
and after that, as drifting smoke allowed,
the desperate blood contention for the Hill.

VI

You, John Ray, who think the Union right,
your children, wife, and servants in the cellar,
safe as can be hoped, take in the fight

for Bloody Hill, as men will call it after
this day makes Oak maiden in its name.
What can you, mile-distant, see (folk hear

the guns for leagues around) of grudging, grim
exchange of ground by men who must appear
as dots, of yards of scrub relinquished, gained

as dots advance, then falter, and fall back,
those which still can, as instinct or command,
or both, require, in acrid air gone thick

with shot, with whizzing balls, and with pierced cries
that drown, at your remove, in din? You watch
dots as Ozark marksmen, slave-free, squint and
      squeeze

the trigger, cut down stout Saint Louis Deutsch
who would, in English, be hard put to own
how what they fled from brings them to this place

to join with Jayhawks certain as John Brown
(perhaps) that God has fingered them for grace,
with boys from Iowa farms, and this state's too,

to strike with great and raw, if doomed bravura,
twice their number of men good and true
as they, God knows, from Arkansas, Missouri,

Louisiana, Texas, even, Brown forbid,
south Kansas, trade lead up and down the hill
until, too few, their general fiercely dead,

they go. And maybe then, John Ray, when all
is done, you turn, and step, quite slow, with care,
past stricken men, some deaf to Southern cheers,

your mind on, who knows, harvest-times before,
on what you have, and hope to have for years,
and bend your knee, and lift the cellar door.

VII

We see it as we can, as time, and earth,
allow. The house behind us, the road winds on.
We pause by placards, scan sunned meadows, stare

at distant stands of trees. The road winds on,
ascends the Hill, and near its crest, we stop,
get out. We rest some seconds, breathing heat,

then slowly move. A sign directs, we walk
a path, and come to, soon, a single cannon,
aimed, it seems, at just bright air. We lay

our hands on its green barrel, hot to touch,
as if just fired. Near here, a placard makes
report, Lyon, wounded, his mount killed,

got astride a proffered other, led on,
turned, waved hat, and met, a volley cracking,
quick, clean doom. We look down, over scrub

and brush, see it, hear it, as we can,
tangled movement, parching shouts, Price,
Old Pap, out front below, shot through flesh

he had to spare, rallying his rag-tags,
wresting blood regard, look to where
McCulloch, cool as Texas, got enough

men into line, beat back Sigel's dawn
attack. Not much stirs, the land lies still
and shimmering in the August sun, vast

and central, the nearest wash of sea, and that
not ocean but a gulf, a crow-fly half
a thousand miles away. The Ray House, its

peaked porch, its roof, its yard, sits small,
in right proportion to the scene that rolls
below. We shade eyes, take it, sweeping, in,

and then begin, back in the car, the slow
descent that leads us out. The asphalt road
gleams silver in the sun, then goes shadowed,

overhung by trees. The Center rounds
again to view, the tortuous circuit comes
complete, we pass on, make retreat to town,

enter onto Battlefield Road, broad
and shadeless, rife with malls, and
food and drink emporiums to daze

the counting eye. We creep in traffic, light
by light, thirsty, hungry, make impulsive choice,
turn of, troop in, commandeer a booth, set

our books and maps beside us, order drink,
and when it comes, stiffen, hoist chill steins,
salute them, as we can, down here, this day.

VIII
By the sevens, grant them praise.

John Ray, praise him, pioneer,
praise the Widow Steele, his wife,
hail their breed, the house they raised.
They intruded, tribes be damned,
cut down trees, made fields, kept slaves.
War pursued, then passed, they stayed,
dwelt a decade more, and died.

Rhoda, Wiley, pale fate's pawns,
chattel, born so, chant them praise.
Own, allow, their earnest lives,
mark what kindness their way came.
Celebrate what did not break,
spirit, all who spring from them.
raise a cold sound, sing them clear.

Nathaniel Lyon, one lean
Yankee, flint the stuff that flecked
his brain. Unforgiving, brave,
ill-tempered, killed, tough soldier,
Union's martyr, yield him praise.
Men with cause to curse him paused,
gave his grave remains respect.

Sterling Price, oak-staunch, praise long
Missouri's man, Virginian
born, doubter of disunion,
loyal to his soil. Lion-
fearless, laughter's friend, "Old Pap"
to his troops, they put trust, fond,
backed him to the bitter end.

Foiled Franz Sigel, sing him too,
Price Napoleon by compare,
laud the solid men he led,
crossed an ocean craving peace,
found war waited, did not wince,
answered to the drum they heard.

Ben McCulloch, Crockett's friend,
tough frontiersman, took his force
to where the fight was, tout him
for it, hail his men, Southrons
bred west of the River, put
to test in torn Missouri,
knowing this: the land: defend.

Praise, Americans, our kin,
trapped in time, in history's vise,
made to choose, when choice they had,
in a damned, and destined, war.
Praise them all, praise them in us,
praise the great bird that soars free,
lofts lone cry, by Wilson Creek.

♦

The above stanzas pay a kind of oblique homage to a 1500-year Welsh bardic tradition, in which praise is seen as the chief end of poetry, and a seven-syllable alliterative line is commonly employed.

From The Road to Shiloh

I

Locations in the Mind

His mind had never let it go. It was
one of a handful of scenes from his
childhood the gathered years had failed

to curtain, or to even shadow down.
There was a pine-wood, high in Colorado,
where he, strayed from camp, had lain for
    an hour

on the thickly needled floor, alone with
filtered sunlight, the scent of resin,
the restless flickering of birds. There was

a trestle bridge in Illinois, shortcut
home to an August cottage, where he and
his mother, hand in hand, making easy time

across the ties, had felt quick fear, begun
to run, although no train was due for hours
There were these scenes, located early on,

that had not gone, or taken later shade.
The April place of guns and stones made one.
It was his father who had seen the sign,

turned on impulse, quit the main road,
miles from anywhere on the way home
from Florida, and brought them to it

as an afternoon declined. It was in Tennessee,
there were meadows and woods, and a languid
curving river, the soft spring sunlight had

felt warm to his touch as he laid his hands
on the bronze of cannon, on monumental,
graven stones, on pyramids of stacked black

balls. It had compelled, the guns and stones,
the fields and trees, the water's tranquil bend,
the black balls piled, in April sun. He knew

that something great and fierce had been
        there,
but what it was, a boy could never say.
A boy could only know it marked his dreams

could only sometimes lie in bed at night
and say the grave old word that was its name
until sleep took him. Hear the name now:
        Shiloh.

II
The Place of Peace

What Hebrews those old Yankees were at heart,
all those dead-right covenanted fathers
with their city on a hill in Massachusetts,

obsessed with sin and mad to show election,
shuck the fear that they were damned, moving on
beyond New England, raising towns and churches

in Ohio, raising rightful hell about the slaves,
though not their closet cargo from the trade;
it should have been a natural for the Yankee

mind to seize it, passing Pittsburg Landing by,
but it was Southern men instead, who said
and kept on saying that it would be known

for the crude log church with the grave old name;
the place of peace, it means, or something
like it, it was where those Hebrews kept their

awful Ark, their casket of the deal of the ages
with Jehovah, their case for Us and Him,
Gentiles take a number, their potent totem-chest

for war; even those great uncut thugs the Philistines
half-bought it, got goose-bumps on their foreskins
when the Hebrews hauled it out, there by Shiloh,

whooping doom; yet Philistines, by damn,
were men too, had the gonad-stuff for war,
showed it big that day by Shiloh, got

high dudgeon up for Dagon, smote the host
of old Jehovah, slew its men and boys
by thousands, sent the Chosen People flying,

carted off the Ark to boot. Dim-eyed prophets
lost their sons, sons went that day like
shreds of a covenant, like Eli's Phinehas,

who left a wife to birth and wail and die,
to cry the glory is departed from Israel,
to name the boy Ichabod, the glory is departed,

the Ark of the Covenant is taken from Shiloh,
the glory is departed from the place of peace.
Three thousand years and a log shack later,

glory got worked over good again in Tennessee,
when Beauregard and Johnston took on Grant
and Sherman, and a hundred thousand men

and boys found out how fierce the thing can get
in woods and fields hard by a rugged hutch
that did for church, and bore a grave old name.

♦

(A Saint Louis saloon-keeper is visited at night in the parlor of his old town house by the ghosts of Generals U.S. Grant and Albert Sidney Johnston, commanders, respectively, of the Union and Confederate forces in the Battle of Shiloh.)

Ghost Talk

I

Grant

Sometimes at night, home from the saloon,
he would sit in the dark parlor of his
old Saint Louis house and perceive the general

in the shadows opposite, slouched at ease
in a great wing-chair, his booted legs
extended, his tunic half undone, the glow

from each slow draw on his diminishing cigar
effecting a tiny, momentary rose
against his blueness in the gloom. Strong spirits

seemed in order on such nights, and so he
always offered, and was not refused.
The general took them now with just a little

ice, and ironically preferred a brand
called Rebel Yell. Never was better whiskey
named in a worse cause, he sometimes declared,

though mostly he just sipped and let that go.
For him Saint Louis was a grand old haunt,
and he liked to reminisce, of how he had courted

Julia at White House, married her in town,
come back to live when he left the Army
failed at farming and the real estate business,

even failed at selling firewood, but found
the bar congenial at the Planters' House Hotel.
And of how he had come back to the city from Galena,

sporting a star, and then gone south to fight,
and all the rest. He liked to talk of those
maiden battles, and always came around

to just the one. It was, he said, least
understood of all. Yes, he had in some ways
been surprised, he knew the rebels were gathering

at Corinth, where the rail lines met, but had
not expected they would venture out to meet
him, strike him at the Landing, in full force,

nor had Sherman; on that they had agreed.
And yes, it was pleasant at the Cherry Mansion,
nine miles down the river at Savannah,

where he could nurse his injured leg, sleep
in a bed, have a drink in his room, take his ease
for a time at the end of evening on the wide

verandah with a last cigar. He'd waited
there for Buell, it was a lovely place. It seemed
a relatively harmless indulgence, after

all the hard times and the obscure years.
And besides, his steamboat was tied up
just below, stoked and ready; it was not that

far to go. When the sound of cannon reached
him at his Sunday breakfast, he was on
the water quickly, on the field by nine.

No, it was not the surprise that mattered,
though he never let that happen again.
It was what came after, to his own mind

and Sherman's. Came, and settled, understood.
After Shiloh, Cable wrote, the South
never smiled. Nor, in truth, said Grant, did we.

II

Johnston

He had known a time would come when
    he would
find them there, not so much awaiting
his return from the saloon as just taking

their nocturnal ease in his parlor,
which had, he was glad, two equally great
wing-chairs. They had helped themselves
    to drinks,

and seemed genially engaged. They barely
paused to acknowledge his entry. Honor,
Grant was saying. That was a noble thing

you did, making your surgeon to stay behind,
and with our men. And if it was reflexive,
more power to you. I met no such test

at Shiloh, if only because, and good luck
too, I wasn't in your boots. You were taking
prisoners, we were falling back, most of that

first day, but for the Hornet's nest. You made
it hot for us, all right. You know I had
my scabbard hit. He studied his cigar. Yes,

said Johnston. If that ball had struck a little
to one side, history would have had you too,
as of that day. And if they'd had to judge

us both on what we'd done till then, you'd not
rate much more notice in the chronicles
than me. Perhaps not, said Grant. Have another

brandy, sir. I doubt it would have mattered
in the end. From where we sit said Johnston,
I have to judge you right. But it might have

taken longer, cost us even more in blood
Your bill was dear enough in Virginia,
but you got it finished in a year. To spare

you at Shiloh may finally have been kind.
Well, said Grant, I did learn hard things there.
But you, had you lived, would have had that too;

you might have balanced what I know. You are
being gallant, sir, said Johnston. I know
you felt I was deficient. And yet I take

you as sincere. You did respect our will
to fight, and suffer, for our cause. But you
wronged us greatly, sir, let's have it out,

when you said that our cause was one of the worst
for which a people ever fought. Grant sipped
his Rebel Yell. General, he said, you fought

to break the Union and to save slavery,
that strikes me as a worst cause two times over.
We fought for our homes, said Johnston. our homes,

our women, our way of life. I spoke the truth
to the men before Shiloh; what we were
defending was all worth fighting for. If you

had broken with us, and we had invaded
Ohio, you would have felt the same. I doubt
you would have talked about a worst cause then.

No, said Grant. It would not have been the same.
It was you, after all, that had the slaves.
Johnston stared into is cup. Sir, he said,

I doubt it could have turned out worse for them.
We would have freed them ourselves by the century's
end, might have got by with less violence

to them since, spared them disillusion, them
and the country the worst of these ghettos.
A terrible word that, never in our lexicon,

but what it has come down to, has it not,
ghettos? It does not seem to me, sir,
that they have much to thank you Yankees for,

all that moral certainty and impatience,
masking hypocrisy. It could be said, sir,
that they would have fared as well without the war.

I doubt that, said Grant. But than we'll never
know. It's done with, sir. What happened,
happened. We did what we did. It's madness

to speculate about these might-have beens.
It's done for us, said Johnston. That I won't
dispute. Still, we figments in old houses

in Saint Louis have got our roles to play;
we need to talk from time to time. And sir:
you surely know there are worse causes now.

♦

A Southern Soldier Answers,
Near the Year 2000

You ask me why I fought; what can I say
(as if the long years since have shed new light),
but that I had to; Make that wash away

if you can do it, tell me that there lay
at heart of it great wrong. You will be right.
I had to fight you; make that wash away,

cast eyes skyward, then look down and play
the card that has you, in my place, contrite.
You ask me why, and what is there to say,

I stood my soil, found I was bound to pay
its blood price whole, come down what hell
   that might.
I had to fight you; make that wash away,

run up your virtues, tramp mine in red clay,
damn my flag as emblem of the night,
then ask me why, and listen to me say
I had to, brother; make that wash away.

       ♦

Price of Virginia:
Missouri's Man

Dawn Tide,
Jamestown, 1611

(The ship draws close; gulls wheel and cry.)
You, John Price, drawn out of Wales,
why have you braved ocean to this place,
this vague, unpromised, threatening land,
which waits a bloody wresting, death by death,
from a people on it for ten thousand
years before Wales ever had a name?
(The ship draws close, the sun cracks cloud.)
What, as water narrows, do you see,
beyond the darkness of massed trees?
It is too soon for you to know
your line will thrive in handsome halls,
masters in a way they would not have
known in Wales; too soon, even,
out of nightmare sleep, to bolt awake, cold-
sweating, freeze the tomahawk's descent.
(Gulls flail, hang fixed, against the wind.)
What can you know? You are dawn's man,
you hope light here will break to west
more large than on the stones of Wales.
(Dark trees loom near; the land comes on.)
John Price, stare hard, take in this air;
what waits your blood here beggars dream.
(The land comes on. The land comes on.)

♦

John Price (the surname is a contraction of "ap Rhys")
was one of the first Welshmen to set foot on American
soil. He became the progenitor of a long line of pros-
perous tobacco planters, first in Virginia, and later, in
the person of seventh- generation scion Sterling Price,
in Missouri. In 1622 he was one of the survivors of an
Indian massacre in which 347 settlers were killed.

The Encounter
Central Missouri, October 1864

He sat his horse upon the hill.
There it lay, the town before him,
the flag of Union flared in sun
atop the Capitol's Roman dome.
He pondered if he had the power
to take it, haul the banner down.
It had been years, he had come far,
owned the battle-scars to prove it,
and the cheers of lean, hard men.
Every sinew in him strained
to give the order, make assault,
and yet he knew that if he won
he might not hold the place for long.
The enemy was still possessed,
as he had been from the start,
of more of every iron war-tool,
save for spirit, and for will.

He put the field-glass to his eye,
looked down more closely on the town
where he had once had charge to govern.
They were there, how many strong
he had no way to surely know,
waiting for him, brave men mostly,
tense behind their works and walls.
He felt a chill race down his spine.

It was no sudden twinge of fear,
he knew what that was, any soldier
did, but something strange, as if
beside him was another, come across
some bridge in time, sharing with him
bonds of blood, and knowledge
of just how it was, the last line drawn,
to take on daunting, alien force,
to lead toward a wakened dream in war,
to win, to lose, to watch the dream
grow small, like some great hawk
that, wings outspread, the current caught,
ascends in widening circles
to the rim of sight, and then drifts down,
comes near again, hovering,
for one crystal moment,
fierce, above a taunting town.

He felt it, and he felt it pass.
He let his hand fall, twisted
in the saddle, and saw nothing
that had not been there before.
He knew then what he had to do.
He turned his mount and, moving,
Gave commands. Leagues of country lay
before him, where good men might yet

be raised, there were towns where bonfires
waited, where his troops would meet
glad cheers. Leagues of country stretched
to westward; hope would most augment
him there. He would press on, try
the heartland, glean what further arms
he could. Westward, somewhere, leaves
drained golden, he would find the battle
finally to be fought. The dream
he had so harbored and embodied,
down three bitter, blood-bought years,
would not end yet, would not die here.

◆

Sterling Price, who was governor of Missouri from 1853-1857, and by 1864 was a major general in the Confederate army, was well aware of his Welsh ancestry.

In October of that year he led a force of 12,000 cavalry into Missouri from Arkansas in an unsuccessful attempt to loosen the Yankee hold on the state.

The imagined presence is that of Owain Glyndwr, the great national hero who led the failed Welsh war for independence of 1400-1415, and who, in October 1401, faced a similar situation, and made a similar decision, on a hill above Worcester.

A Touch of Wales

Mountain Spring Song
Snowdon Range, North Wales

A white combustion rules these fields,
and testifies to men, and rams;
the mind of winter thaws, and yields—
great God, the world is drunk with lambs.

The high gray stone is clean of snows,
the streams come tumbling, far from dams,
the wind is green, the day's eye grows—
great God, the world is drunk with lambs.

The heart, gone light as all the ewes,
redounds with milk, and epigrams
that make no sense, except their news—
great God, the world is drunk with lambs.

In gold October, grown to size,
they'll know the hook, and hang with hams,
but March is all their enterprise—
great God. The world is drunk with lambs.

♦

The Wise Cows

The wise cows, in rain,
rise to the crest of the hill
like mottled flotsam and suspend,
heads down, in the lee of the hedge
beneath the thatch of branch and leaf
the wind has scalloped on from sea.
The cows are wise. They are wise
as grass. They are full of butter.
They are the weather. They are ours.

♦

The Cockle Man

They'd had the red tide in
California, and our friends
had written ahead, starved

for cockles and mussels,
asking if Molly Malone
ever hustled Llansteffan;

they were good friends, so we
asked the postmistress, and she
said well, there was this man

in the council houses who still
tried, now and then; we went
to him and he threw up his

hands and said Duw!* cockles were
past tense, like Llywelyn Fawr;*
my wife's face fell like the last

bell Sunday but she said all right,
we'd just take mussels, then;
wait, he said, there may be

one place, up the river; no
promises, mind; the day
before they came he rode up

to our house on his bike
rubber leggings white
with flecks of tide, produced

a sack of mussels, then a larger,
with cockles enough to gorge
a choir of gulls; charged us

a pound; keep the faith, he said.

♦

*Duw=God

*Llywelyn Fawr. Welsh ruling prince, died 1257.
 Fawr=Great

Dai, Live

Prytherch* is dead. We have no right
to doubt it, let alone dispute. We must
contend with men we have in sight,

like Dai* here, who is clean
as dirt. The rumor in the pub
is that he hasn't been seen

out of that ripening outfit
since the Investiture.* It may
be a form of protest, though it

seems more likely, ten pints down,
he's just too whipped to shuck that
wing-grey coat, every button gone,

peel those frazzling sweaters, rife with him
and earth, let those grime-stiff trousers
fall, or try to fall, before things dim.

Too whipped, perhaps, to kick those mud-
brindled boots to a corner, or toss
that crust of a cap to a bed-

post, if he has one. No farmer, Dai,
he digs around the village, roads,
sewers, God knows what, digs all day,

digs everywhere, turns up pints,
grubs of coins for the slot, studies men
who commute to Carmarthen, nods, squints,

grunts a little rugby, weathers at his end
of the bar like a cromlech, drones
like the surf when those with more voice bend

the last elbow in hymn, leaves alone
with a guttural wave, boulders into night,
a man-shape hulking like an age of stone,

that knows no women, but lives with what it
    knows,
hard as breath, or a December rose.

◆

*Prytherch. Iago Prytherch, a Welsh peasant figure in
the poetry of R.S. Thomas, perhaps he greatest Welsh
poet to write in English in the 20th Century. Thomas
announced Prytherch's death in a poem in 1966.

*Dai. A kind of generic name for working-class Welsh-
men, like Paddy for Irishmen.

*Investiture. The installation of the 21-year old Charles
Windsor as so-called Prince of Wales in 1969.

The Holy Well

We walked down the beach at dusk
for a mile and a half, the shrunken
tidal Tywi on our left, around
the darkening points, our feet hardly

knowing the tautly rippled sand, gulls
thinning out, to the path to the well.
My wife was winded. She took to a bench,
gathering breath for home, while I led

our son, eight that day and pure
Missouri, up the soft, dark path.
A gate, and down stone stairs and there
it was, a Gothic arch, its symmetry

gone, set low in the bank at our
feet. That's not a well, he said.
It is, it is, and there must
have been a hermit once, I told him.

Then let me jump in. No, it's too
deep. He tossed a stick. See, it's not
far, the water's just there.
And so it was, black as loam, as

a sound in fresh night. It's not
a well, he said. There's no bucket.
It's been a long time, I said,
besides, it was more a place to go,

like your hideout under the bush near
the alley in Saint Louis. He looked
around, felt the stone. bent and tossed
a second sprig. Then we sat down.

♦

The Drought

A friend, a poet, wrote me near the end
of summer there had been a drought
in Wales; hoarding for the roses,

water off between ten and six, things
like that. I hardly believed it,
it seemed like news of a blizzard

in Death Valley; but he spoke
dry truth; two weeks of sun in
September, sails blazing on the Tywi,

reading in a garden warm with stone,
going barefoot like we'd never left
Missouri; yikes, I said, if this

keeps up we'll be breaking out the mandolins,
taking siestas on the dike, drinking ouzo,
pinching girls' behinds at the market;

of course it didn't; today the rain
drives in from sea as dense as Calvin's
breath, as a five-sharp hymn; only

the very close is green, slate
interposes, windows fog, the wind
tests every crevice and the land,

Welsh land, is wet, dissenting, glad.

♦

Searching the Scriptures

Lot: Some Speculations

I mean what
did he do? One
minute there she

was, flesh of his
flesh, hustling
along beside

him, anxious
as ice-cubes to
get away from

all that fire
and justice
on the plain,

and the next
she's a pillar
of wrath-

solid salt; it
was a hell
of a price,

even if her
curiosity was
morbid; what

did he do? you
could make a
case for not

even break-
ing stride, but
after all, it

was his wife; he
may have carved
a quick R.I.P.,

not looking
back, before
goosepimpling

on, or something
more sober-
ing, like BEWARE;

she may have
become a
kind of sodium-

chloride Ozymandias;
more likely she
wound up ground

♦

Let's Hear It for Goliath

who never asked
to be born
either, let alone
grow nine feet

tall and wind
up a metaphor;
fat chance he
had of avoid-

in the shove
from behind;
his old man
no doubt gave

him a sword
to teethe on,
and a scout
for the Philistine

host probably
had him under
contract by
the end of

junior high;
it was a fix;

and who wouldn't
have cursed

at the sight
of that arr-
ogant runt with
the sling, who,

for all his
psalms, would later
buy one wife
with a hundred

bloody pecker-
skins, and another
with a King's X
on Uriah; bah,

let's hear it
for Goliath, a big
boy who got
bad press but

who did his job,
absorbed a flukey
shot, and died
with a thud.

◆

The Place Where Two
Great Rivers Meet

(This is the sixth and final poem of a sequence covering a journey from the village of Llansteffan in west Wales to Saint Louis, Missouri. A kind of great circuit is completed in that west Wales is warmed by the Gulf Stream, which is fed by the Mississippi River.)

To Where Great Rivers Meet

The final leg at last, I am wedged between
two soldiers, a black boy from Arkansas,
a white from Tennessee, shut of the Rhineland,

talking a streak, we are the journey's final
confederates, to whom the war that mattered
    most
had names like Shiloh and Chickamauga,

and Appomattox at the last. The chance we know
still bleeds alive straight from it, who laugh
together now, one whose ancestors came chained,

one whose trekked the Gap with Boone, and one
whose German grandads got there just before
the guns. We all go west, and south, to home.

Our easy talk goes muted as we come down
from the north, through summer skies unbroken
but for scattered wisps of cloud, to confront

the glacial living fact of level Illinois.
Mister Lincoln's prairies lay out now before
us in great rectangles of gold and green,

dotted with barns and white frame houses,
and here and there the cluster of a town,
the heartland, immense in its shimmering

fecundity. Then, in the distance, a glimpse
of winding water, the Missouri, nearing
consummation of its descent from the West,

across two thousand miles of Indian names,
Dakota, Nebraska, Iowa, Kansas, to conjoin
the Father of Waters for a thousand more,

and sea. We witness union from five thousand feet,
the great brown wedded river now flows south
before us, winding, flexing, toward the Gulf,

to feed the stream that warms Llansteffan's shores.
It sure is something, says the boy
from Tennessee. One hell of a river,

his black companion adds. More river, boys,
I think than hell can know. Saint Louis looms,
gray bridges, the leaping, gleaming Arch.

◆

Festa Italiana

For Lawrence "Yogi" Berra, son of The Hill

Hordes of autumn gapers jam The Hill
today; wagons from the ranch-housed County,
cars from flattened Illinois, clog these little

streets, that but for names of shops and *ristoranti*,
could never, in the maddest voyeur's dream,
masquerade as *strade*; no; these runty

houses, salami with roofs,were built to ream
tax-men, keep their frontage proscuitto-thin;
no banished *professori* in the teem

that clotted here, sloughed *poveri* to a man;
Genoa, Turin, Venice, Florence, Rome—
names in travel folders to the short, thick kin

who tend these shallow gutters, nurse these trim
green mats of lawn; these are the scions
of the lava-larded soil, whose patron hymn

implored the donkey's saint, ignored the lion's,
whose *nonni*, poor as flint and sweat, heard the blast
of huge noon whistles, dreamt of stack-spired Zions,

found them here. Years go; softball is their best
game now, not *bocce*, and they drink more lager beer
than dago red; they've prospered; half, at most,

still work with their hands; their sons find bigger
homes in Wildwood, come back to sip on Sundays,
fondly, as now; they watch *mamma* finger

gnocchi in street stalls, and when *pappa* plays
the concertina, they sing; they join the line
for mostaccioli at the church, and they gaze,

with us, near Berra Park, at the mud-dull ton
of the statue of The Immigrants, bulking squat
and rude as pig-iron; *e La Santa Famiglia*, done,

they think, with steerage, heads up, hope-sot,
eyes as vastly glazed as faith; the man's hat batters
down around his ears; dumpy madonna, fraught

with shawl, bulks against him, clutching what matters,
the child; it's rigged, lachrymose, baldly hints
at opera bathos, yet the cold eye all but waters,

and foundry gates, at dark, seem kind, as glints
of harvest ghost-moon gloss our inching cars,
while crones on porches rock their last drowsed stints,

gray men gargoyle steps of sabbathed bars,
and cross *bambini* cry beneath first stars.

◆

Sommernachtstraum
for the Bayrische Bier Stube

This is still German turf;
 houses in tight
rank on broomed sidewalks
 doorsteps scrubbed right

down to 1880;
 no condemned signs here,
where red brick and white stone,

This is still German turf;
 houses in tight
rank on broomed sidewalks
 doorsteps scrubbed right

down to 1880;
 no condemned signs here,
where red brick and white stone,
 given kinder care,

endure; schule, kirche,
 altenheim, stand,
markers of sane men
 who quit a damned land,

its jackboots, spiked helmets
 and dueling-scar steel,
and brought their old Teuton hound
cleanly to heel.

Oom pah-pah, oom pah-pah,
 tubas presume
that always and ever shall
 beer gardens bloom;

ja, ja, ja, liebfraumilch
 melt darkness, melt;
clean corner taverns shall
 lantern die welt.

kartoffel pfannkuchen,
 sauerbraten, kraut,
foaming on fathers' laps
 kinder sing out

for nips at the lager,
 pale gold as the moon
that tubas its oom pah-pah
 sommernacht tune.

We come down, tourists,
 to these solid blocks,
so snug on the South Side,
 where grandfathers' clocks

tick pendulous order,
 and rot is kaput,
where Schwarz is a last name
 and black men are moot,

where Gott in his Himmel
 believes in the strong,
who will what they are
 and who earn their night's song,

and rise and join wildly,
 our steins drooling foam,
and at the last prosit
 slosh, bloat-bellied, home.

♦

A Honky in the New St. Louis Census, 2019

Winter;
driving a rising exit curve
from a strip that cuts
to suburbs from the park, I trail
a city truck, grey as the day;
it grinds the overpass in low,
spewing rock salt blue as robins' eggs
onto concrete gone to glaze.
 Aboard,
a black man (half
his city now) burgeons at the knees
from a glittering, grainy ton, muscling
azure shovelfuls onto the salter's maw;
his lemon slicker, leaking light like spring,
blazons him in motion
through the steady freezing rain.

♦

Where Does the South Begin?

Down to Memphis

Where does the South begin, how do you know
when you're there? And do you care? He did,
having grown to young manhood in the region

of Saint Louis, a place which seemed to have
something to do with it, For all its
solid Germans and their beer, its serious

winters, laced with ice, the feel of the city
in the end was Southern, What tilted things
to South was summer; then the place was just

too hot and steamy, prone to thunderstorms
of afternoons, too lush with succulent
weeds and vines, with trees that dangled languid

pods, too full at evening of the deafening
thrum of insects, to ever pass for north,
all wintry chills be damned. And then this, too:

drive south for just a bit and you will know
you are getting there. Waitresses drawl,
grits is on the menu, rockers are ubiquitous

on roadside porches, junker cars are nearly
so in yards, and the lolling men in denim
in the squares of towns are men who speak

of different dirt from Iowa, whether you can
hear their words or no. Thirty miles or so
and the line has been crossed; everything

sooth of that is gravy.
                    Now, off the old road,
cruising the interstate, he had passed over,
the plain of the River never far on his left,

the Ozarks rolling hazy off to his right.
In an hour or so the hills had receded,
he was into the Boot Heel, Swamp East as

home folks call it, cotton fields and all.
Arkansas then, flat with rice and beans,
clear to Memphis, which like Saint Louis,

rises grandly from the River, towering
over bridges. The tall, glittering building
stood close to the bridge-end, and was surely

the ultimate Holiday Inn,
                              He found
the lobby teeming with exuberant blacks.
There were substantial matrons tip to toe

in white satin, in uniform, almost, except
for their hats, which ranged from the demure
to the semi-spectacular. Their consorts,

men in suits of black, deacon-like in dignity,
solid with authority, exuded a benevolent,
almost jocund, sobriety. Around these figures,

magisterial, half-Olympian, swirled their young,
vivacious, chattering, brightly dressed,
and perhaps aspiring, in their own good time,

to elevation to the white and black.
They were, said the hotel's sign of welcome,
the Apostolic Church of Jesus Christ,

which struck him as pure Gospel truth.
                                    He made
his way through, ascended to his room,
surrounded by a cloud of women in white satin,

matriarchal angels, who laughed and smiled.
In a column of glass their car rose slowly,
he looked down on the city, the River moving,

the lights of the bridges, the park at Mud
Island, tiny cars and people in the streets,
The Peabody, the Grand Old Hotel of the South,

or so they called it now, looking its refurbished
part a block or so away. He felt beatific,
an angel by osmosis, and departed with

reluctance, bowing to the matrons as the doors
eased closed.
                    Later, in the lobby,
pondering dinner, he sat on a sofa, sipped a martini,

the crush of black sanctity, or virility,
or both, or more, all-powerful around
him. They walked and talked and laughed,

drank Coca-Colas and lemonade, called
to their young if they grew too boisterous,
and did not seem to mind that he had gin.

In a corner a grand piano, Japanese,
played such things as tunes of Cole Porter,
meant for cocktail hours, all by itself,

and badly. Little children gathered to it,
giggling and whispering, touching, as they
dared, the computer-driven keys. Ain't this

something, boomed a generous voice behind him.
'This place full of the brothers and sisters.
Ain't this something. Where you get that drink?

♦

Poem in October
Great Smoky Mountains, Tennessee

Splashed with blazing ash and maple hues,
golds and crimsons, deep-fired oaken tones,
the mountain beckons something in our bones.
There is no trail that we are free to choose,
this high-sunned day, but one we know will bend
for hour on hour in ever-steepening ways
to get the crest, and lay before our gaze
autumnal ridges rolling without end.

And so it seems, when having met its raise,
the mountain's long demand on heart and lung,
six thousand feet, we stand on stone among
last trees, and view what strains to call forth
    praise,
or its close kin: great smoke that owes no fire,
a blue-gray haze, like sea, through which they
    thrust,
bright forest islands, rising as if just
proclaimed, by lords of color and desire.

We take it in, not lords but men who must
account to muted truth along the track,
vacant cabins, with at times out back,
ragged little burial stones which trust
that some god, somewhere, knows the knife-
    scratched name,
more like that not that of a quick-gone child,
which wind and rain have long since reconciled
with blankness, and the mountain's prior claim.

We came, made rock-bound home, and finally filed
down from the high hard fastness to become.
the folk of towns, and fields that do not numb
the heart with dreams of stones yet to be piled;
the mountain streams we drank from tumble on,
and brush by, sometimes, mill-wheels at a loss
for work to do but serve the needs of moss,
or mind a passer of life turned, and gone,

as turning now, our sight in sweep across
this smoked expanse where blazoned ridges flare,
oak and ash and maple blast to air
great autumn's fanfare nothing can emboss,
bright with dying, and the reason we
have toiled to stand here, and, atop last stones,
embrace the mountain's hardness in our bones,
alive and glad, on high, in Tennessee,

♦

The Man Who...

The Man Who Forgot He Ate His Lunch
Gaslight Square, Saint Louis

Why some old jazz men live as long
as Moses beats me cold; I mean you
kind of get it with the classical

cats, regular hours, not a lot of
booze, no-smoke joints to play in,
sacked out by midnight after the gig;

the man who gets his kicks in soup and fish.

Okay, so he was not always with it,
damn few geezers that old are,
but my guess is while he was gone

he blew jazz in his head; hey, it was
cool that he was here at all,
he'd played great sax but last I

heard that never fixed a liver; he
was kind of a riff on legs, up
and down the street all day, belting

a shot or beer in every joint,
and maybe his lunch too for
all I know, bur I mean it's the

gospel that he always ate it here.

Lunch is lunch is lunch is lunch,
I mean who cares how many times
you do the number, as long as you're

still hungry and your credit is good;
I never got my back up when he
forgot he ate it, I mean it isn't

like we dish up gourmet chow; when
he'd ask me had he had it I'd
just tell him yeah, and offer him a

meatball on the house; no thanks, mac,
he'd say, I just want to know; hit
me one more time before I go; I say

the day he dropped that man blew jazz.

those guys work, but not like a jazz
man, night after night till the fat
broad wings it, smoking it out, hot sounds

and cool, and hitting the hard stuff
right along; I mean your jazz dude
on the average kicks off years before.

♦

The Man Who Detested
Red Fire Engine Endings

You've got to avoid the red fire engine
ending or the whole of your story
will go up in smoke; the gratuitous

bump-off is a factor of life, but will
not do to resolve a fiction, even
in New Jersey; so he'd said for years,

since the student story of the dentist
from Weehawken who, sick of halitosis
and his corpulent wife, was on his way

home to talk the terms of his extraction,
his farewell to floss, when splat!
a red fire engine slams around the corner

and lays him out flat as a tube of used
Colgate; it doesn't work, he'd said; you've
got to face the fatso wife; otherwise a column

just topples on Oedipus, Macbeth slips on a
    haggis
and flails down from Dunsinane, and Ahab
chokes on salt pork the night before the whale.

Term had gone, and his report was in.
The red engine within him would not run
long. It was a family thing, he had hoped

it might come later, but that was not on.
It was not absurd, or even unfair,
it was just biology, and a truth

of his story. He read it right enough,
yet could not stand that he should end
deficient as a fiction, just too sick,

like some pathetic diva whose bacilli
stop the song. He had seen the firehouse
near the hospital complex, the great

ironic engines, latent in the shade.
He knew the city, full of false alarms,
would not keep him half a day. One would come

his way, in a fierce intent cacophony of siren
and klaxon, and he would tense, as if
to spring. And so he did, and was resolved

♦

The Man Whose Head Was Full of Tunes

I

His head was always host to a tune.
It was not the same tune always,
but always a tune. At times it was

simply something catchy from the charts,
at others an inevitable progression
of Beethoven, a cool jazz elegance,

a clarity of Bach, a thrum of calypso,
an old Welsh air, an operatic march,
it was anything at all, but it was always

a tune. The tunes struck up at waking,
accompanied his day, muted reluctantly
into sleep, resumed if he should rouse

in some cold corner of the night. He had
not more choice than a violin. he was
purely instrumental. The impetus was
    strange.

II

In time he saw people hum to themselves,
absently drum their arthritic fingers
when reason had taken its final bow

and gone, and knew it might be so with him.
To go that way seemed more all right than mad,
there seemed a logic to it for a man

whose head was tuned, and when the logic failed,
a kid of gladness stuck, which had to do
with what he owed to rhythm, to a pulse

in space, a metronomic force, that drove
an elemental fugue that lent its beat
to life, and let him move his while in time.

It seemed all right. He even came to dream
an obscure maestro held him in in regard,
and led him towards a colder, stranger tune.

♦

The Man Who Needed to See the Sikosky

Miss Dallas the prep cook was a good church
lady, who, when excited, chopped fresh words.
When she had cupped an earful of lascivious

hints of Jackson the porter's organic nights,
she let him have it, cleaver-quick:
Jackson, you is sick! You jest don't think
right, boy! You needs to see the Sikosky!

It was
all good sport, for Jackson at least,
who did the hard work, never showed up drunk,

and whose fun was mostly clean as his
exuberant virility. And so he
laughed, and kept on teasing. It was the white

boss who, his salad years subsiding, began
to brood on what she'd said. He'd caught
the word Miss Dallas had made mince of,

had sometimes thought of seeing such a man,
yet knew in his gut it would just cost him
money, as what ate at him there was not

a couch affair. Still, what her mangling
now dangled engaged him: might there not be,
in his dream, the Sikosky?

                      It was a dream
he'd had for years, of being lost at night
in the deep black of the ghetto, wandering

urgently down vacant, littered streets,
past boarded houses where no light shone,
where arc-light on corners shed their

luminance on nothing, and yet where
something, just in shadow, moved. He knew
it was in part a dream of madness

of sheer being, configured to the time
and place in which he had to live. That, and
race too. It was an American dream.

And as it was
his dream, he wished he could augment it,
compel it beyond confusion and cold sweat.

He wished that he could dream it, corners stopped,
the final run-down block before him,
the sign, in a dingy upper window,

neon-lurid, glowing like a word; SIKOSKY.

Then, like that, a fake, a dodge, and he might
do it, slip the shadow, race up creaking,
rotted stairs, and face a door where gold light

leaked. Then, he might hear it, a deep enduring
voice, resonant as Africa, and kind.
It's all right, boy; it's done with; come on in.

He could not dream it, though. He woke in time.

◆

Remembered

A Clutch Conjunction

Middle of the freeway, doing sixty-five,
I felt a sudden loss of speed. God,
I thought, I could cause a crash, and maybe

get myself and worse, contingent strangers
killed. As if He'd heard, an exit loomed.
Signaling, braking, every move a cringe,

I made it to the ramp and coasted down,
stopping, finally, on a grassy verge
to slump there, panting, innards in a churn.

A tapping at the window turned my head.
The man, with a reddish, white-flecked beard,
was short but rugged, leathery, tanned,

at sixty-some my junior by a good
two dozen years. A silver pickup sat
behind, shrouded objects in its bed.

I can smell it, he said. Your clutch is shot.
You look like you could use some help. I could,
I said, my phone is on the fritz. No sweat,

he answered. Mine is good. I culled my wallet,
fed him cards; he made the necessary
calls. Done, he gave a little nod and helped

me from my crippled car. We stood together,
talking, in spring sun. Spent twenty years
in the Army, he said, played the role of father

for a dozen kids, two of which the lab says
were my own. Now I mainly do odd jobs.
His voice was deep, but lively, like his eyes.

A tow truck and my son arrived. He met
them with a summary, then came back to me.
When I said, "Can I give..." he cut me short,

thrust forward his right hand. Then as if no
words could add, he turned to his truck, and drove
away. His plate flashed by me: G SAM 2.

♦

*If there are no dogs in heaven, then when I die
I want to go where they went.* —Will Rogers

A Dog Gone

He had some wolfhound, so the shelter said;
he looked the part, but was just half half the size.
He was found wandering in a city park,
thin, coat matted, trailing a short lead.
How he got there stayed unknown;perhaps
his owner had been stricken on a walk,
and as the ambulance sped off, he had been
left behind, alone. Or perhaps he was taken
to the park with reluctance by someone
who no longer could provide, and left there,
with his leash intact, in hope a Samaritan
might pass goodly by.

However it was,
he wound up at the shelter, where he stayed
five weeks, had a bath, regained some weight,
got brushed and groomed. The wife, a volunteer
who walked him, became immediately
his fan. He would stop and turn, as they moved
along, then cock his head and catch her eye,
as if to say, "I'm with you; and it's good".

It was only a matter of time before,
the papers signed, he jumped into their car,
plopped down on the back seat, and heaved
what seemed a gruntled sigh. When they reached
    home
he leapt right out, and dragging leash, dashed
right up to their front door. It was not long
before they felt that he had somehow lived
there always; he took his ease in every room,
and slept at night beside their bed, except
when he ensconced upon it. They gave him
an Irish name, McGee, and at times in winter,
as he lay by the fire, they could have sworn
they were in Tara's Hall.

                He shared their life
for thirteen years, went with them everywhere,
romps in the park, vacations in the mountains,
dinners at outdoor cafes. Then, one day,
a week before Christmas, he just lay down
and ceased to eat. They sat up with him
four bleak nights; neither they nor the vet
could do a thing. Then, without a whimper,
lying by the fire, he went to where it is
dogs go. To where, pulled after, we go too.

♦

A Modern Poet
circa 1970

Life went well; he had begun to publish
here and there, little mags, and had
landed a job at a good small college.

Then, not long into autumn term,
he was asked to read at the Luncheon Coterie,
a cultural fixture in the leafy old town.

The woman who approached him went
right to the point. "As a modern poet
you do read with lighting, music, all that

sort of thing, don't you?" she inquired,
a note of assumption in her tone. "Beats me,"
he was tempted to reply, but as a new hire

at the college he refrained, and instead
answered blandly, "I'll see what I can do.
He found tree students, one who played

guitar, another the bongo drums, and one who,
a theater major, had done some lighting.
They met to rehearse in a college studio,

and came to the conclusion they did best,
so to speak, with a lengthy poem sequence
called "I Dreamt of the Angel of Death

in Kansas City." Despite all the practice
he still found it distracting, when performance
day came due, to be swathed in various

pastel hues, and to have to speak at times
at stentorian volume to overcome the strums
and drumbeats, and as regards the business

of the Angel of Death, the intermittent moaning
of the bongo girl. He could hear the women
shuffling in their seats, but when it was done

they applauded politely, expressed their thanks,
and laid on quite a pleasant lunch, which, while
     tasty,
would have gone better with a good stiff drink.

♦

An Old Father's Tale

It was a task to bring a father joy,
concocting nightly stories for a daughter
who, arrived in bed, a brightness in her eye,

banked on him for transport down the road
to Nod. His plots lurched Gothic, a lurking villain
always, an Evil Ed, a Slithering Sid,

out to strip her cruelly of some worn, loved thing,
and when the dastard, mid-tale, had prevailed,
she would clutch her pillow, wincing, as if stung.

But not for long: stout champions were on call,
and one quite soon would send the blackguard
    packing,
thwarted, sputtering vengeful oaths. The doll,

the blanket, the stuffed panda, hers once more,
the night light on, she then could start to drowse,
wrapped warm again in knowledge of her sure

protection, by the likes of Stonewall Jackson,
Davy Crockett, Sherlock Holmes, the Wizard
Merlin, Prince Llywelyn, and Bill the Moon Man,

high on circus stilts. Time seemed suspended,
often, then. Now, his daughter decades gone,
he sits some nights in her old room, surrounded

by the cadre he had once employed, as Crockett buffs
his long gun, Jackson strokes his sword,
Llywelyn murmurs princely Welsh, Merlin laughs,

then hushes, Holmes puffs pensive in the gloom,
and Bill the Moon Man, house-tall, peers in
from outside. It is good; he is glad to have them

there, to know his figments have remained
on call, ready still for service in some father's
tale, stalwarts of the wry, paternal mind,

and champions to the finish of the storied
room, where things of worth abide defended
as thought embraces what all story bends toward.

◆

Winter; The Park

We watched from the cindered alley as the
couple came out of the cold and the dark
into the brief intercession of light

at the corner and passed in their whispering,
arm in arm, into the mysterious
winter thing that was the Park. We were three boys,

turned thirteen and compelled to be curious.
moved by what was stirring in our just
pubescent loins, out to uncover what

wonder we could on a Saturday night
in the pocked and gritty town before
the steel mill whistle blew and sent its great

bass curfew, like some hollow groan of earth,
ascending and diffusing towards the stars.
We followed them, or what we took for them,

one shadow, moving, intermittently visible,
down the entry path between the leafless trees,
the somber clumps of shrub and evergreen,

uncertain in the night. The path was hard
and black beneath our feet. We crossed a small
bridge that arched a frozen pond, and in

the central garden's maze of rock and hedge,
we lost them. No shadow made a move
upon the field beyond. We stood there, silent,

listening to the wind. Its moan was constant,
clean and cold. It was old. The distant entry light
was dim. The curfew blew. We ran, and ran.

♦

The Pentecostal Duck

They were three boys in early teen years, stock
of merchant fathers in the dark, steel-furnaced
    town,
out for a lark on a Sunday night in June.
In the sack one carried was a fat white duck.

The church was a place for people from the hills,
hard folk, bred in Tennessee, drawn in due
    course
to the Mississippi, to labor on the hearth-floors
of the mill. They lived in drab near-hovels

on the wrong side of the tracks, they were loathe
to suffer trespass, swift with fists if crossed,
Their faith was a queer business at its best,
judged townsmen, they were said to writhe and
    mouth

weird sounds, and sometimes handle living snakes.
Their house of worship was a clapped affair,
unsteepled, squat, dwarfed by the lone sycamore
that reared in its dirt yard; its white paint flaked,

its windows were clear glass. "We'll wait a while
behind there", one boy said. He'll call on the
    Spirit,
then they'll start to moan. That's when we'll do it,
heave the duck in. Heave the duck, and run like hell".

They edged, in shadow, round the back. Light blazed
from open windows, a hot, breeze stirred. There was
murmuring within. Soon, a strong male voice
came on. It droned, then flared, and as if seized,

implored the Ghost; chairs moved, there was a cry,
they heard a guttural moan; one boy bent, taut,
and grasped the duck. He felt the quickening beat
beneath breast feathers. The moans increased; he

flung it in. There were shouts, a scrambling row,
a thud, a squawk, and silence. The boys stood
frozen. Then, of a sudden, like a pent thing freed,
the sound of birdsong filled the night. They saw,

out front, a white shape rising, slender, graceful,
past dark leaves. As the boys fled panting down
the road, one heard, he swore, though he told no one,
a joyful gibberish rampant in his soul.

◆

The Elm Bush

You've got to prune your therefores at a time
like this; Frost was right about the need
of being versed vis-a-vis the country,
and Shakespeare, of course about the folly

of false compare; those thank a green plant
bumper stickers, like a lot of bumper stickers,
border on the sticky; and when one of my
sophomore girls, after reading Wordsworth,

wrote about holding hands with an old
oak tree, I gagged; so when Tom the tree man
wanted to chain-saw the little "ell-um"
after he did the job on the dying weeping

willow in the back yard two years ago
it was no dice then simply because where
it grew, through alley brick by the front stoop,
was my small son's hideout; the foundation

can take it a while yet, I told him; this
May, when the deaf handyman who lays
brick well and does most other things all
right finished patching the front walk he

finger-talked the thing to death; my son had
outgrown his hideout, and I gave the nod;
he axed it quick for eight bucks and I missed
it for a while, but from the stoop at night

I could see more play of shadow on the brick,
so I forgot it; now, the ides of August on us,
damned if the thing hasn't burst out big
as plastic, shut of itself to its root,

with elm leaves quivering huge as my hand.

♦

Beethoven at the Alamo
and Other Poems

(After a dispute between Charlie Brown and Schroeder in the comic strip "Peanuts", in which Schroeder is finally forced to assert that Beethoven, too, was at the Alamo.)

Beethoven at the Alamo

In the on-
going because
essential

argument as to
who was the
greater man,

Beethoven or
Davy Crockett,
one must

consider it,
suppose he
hadn't died,

suppose it's
nine years on,
there he is,

in his study
in Vienna,
working on

an even later
string quartet,
when poof!

it's the Alamo,
brick-shards
and piano

splinters flying,
Crockett and
the buckskin

men hell-bent
for doom
around him,

out of lead,
slashing with
Bowie-knives,

flailing with
long guns,
dark soldados

everywhere,
upending his
piano, putting

his score to
the bayonet,
Gott im Himmel,

Wellington's
Victory was
never like this,

the northern
force is not
sufficient here,

the last man
in buckskin
goes down,

kaput, only
an ersatz
gringo stands,

the conscript
campesinos
pause, Santa

Anna comes,
what will he
make of the

huge-browed
extranjero
with the wild

hair, the
dude clothes,
deaf as brass,

oblivious to
command
babbling in

a guttural
tongue not of
the Yanqui,

shaking his
fist at
fire and ruin,

or is it at
the alien
hills beyond?

No importa;
leave him;
there is blood

that matters
to be let at
Goliad, and a

rendezvous with
vengeance at
the stream of

San Jacinto;
leave him;
he is not yet

part of what
has happened
here; leave him

to smoke and
rubble, the
stench of death,

the vulture,
the coyote,
and the coming

night, leave him
to this famous,
empty place,

leave him to
the vastness
of the Texas

dark, let him
stop it, take
its measure,

fit what keys
to it he can, let
him make its

great black
ranges move,
and sound his

cold lone star.

♦

The Least of These

A centipede scrambles
in my kitchen sink,
desperate to ascend

its sides. I stop tap,
catch him on a slip
of paper, lift him out

and flick him clear.
Counter gained, he
legs it safe away.

An earthworm wriggles
on the hot concrete,
stranded in the after-

shower sun. I pick him,
with a grimace, up,
walk him inland twenty

yards, drop him down
in tree-shade on still
rain-damp, grassy soil.

A bee got in the sun-porch
buzzes at a window,
stymied by the stubborn

fact of glass. I trap her
in a plastic cup,
cap it with a cocktail

coaster, lift that in
the garden, watch her zip
toward bright blooms.

A Monarch flutters in
from darkness
through an open

kitchen door, wafts
erratic round the room.
I set my fork down,

scrounge a candle,
light it, switch
off, lure her out.

Lord, let them count.

♦

Handyman

My name is Ed Landers. I occur. I
look after your summer house in New Hampshire
in the winter, report the troublesome
news when thieves break in. I put up chain-link
fence around your parking slab to protect
your car from porcupines. I fill you in
on birth and death, divorce and scandal,
other village doings when you come in June.
I am your connection. I saw your fire-
wood and run you a pipe from the creek
to your kitchen sink. I have other names.
When you come, in and out of English novels,
up from London to Wales you call me

Hugh Halfbacon, Jones the Fixit, or Good
Old Dai. I connect more, there. I
have puttered longer in the stones. I
am a stone, my scratchings indecipherable,
good to lean on. I take care of your
cottage up the coombe, so that when you have
your divorce or breakdown you can come clean
in a wild and proper place before you
go back, as you must. I live and die and
suffer just like you, or so you sometimes think,
but my literary utility would diminish
if I did not remain vague,
like Faulkner's Dilsey. I am Faulkner's Dilsey.
I am not even here. This is your voice.

♦

For the Dun Dove

A bird that serves to sign the Spirit may
not always come on wings that are pure white.
the mourning dove draws color from our clay.

And neither need it bear us down a spray
from up there somewhere out of mortal sight;
a bird that serves to sign the Spirit may

grub for its substance in an alley-way,
or, flushed afield, brave bursts of shot in flight.
The mourning dove draws color from the clay

of our chanced earth, the charge it must obey
is just to try, each day, another night.
A bird that serves to sign the Spirit may,

though pale against the raven, come to play
a part as dark, depending on the light.
The mourning dove draws color from our clay

that springs life new from prior life's decay,
as on the ground that grants to it the right
a bird that serves to sign the Spirit may.
The mourning dove draws color from our clay.

♦

About the Author

JON DRESSEL passed away in April 2024 while putting the final touches on this collection of verse. He was a versatile and prize-winning poet in both English and Welsh. A dairyman, college teacher, and pub proprietor in Saint Louis, Dressel spent some years in Wales, pursuing an interest in ancestors. He mastered the language, history, and spirit of the Welsh. He was a patriot and bard of Missouri and Wales, both troubled borderlands. His poetic subjects were not only historical. He was uniquely imaginative and a poignant observer of private life.

Dressel's books include *Out of Wales: Fifty Poems, 1973-1983, Rhubanau Dur (Ribbons of Steel), The Road to Shiloh* and *Wyneb yn Wyneb (Face to Face).* The latter, a discussion of Welsh nationalism, has an image of R.E. Lee on its cover.

Available From Green Altar Books

If you enjoyed this book, perhaps some of our other titles will pique your interest. The following titles are now available for your reading pleasure… Enjoy!

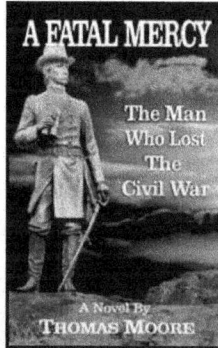

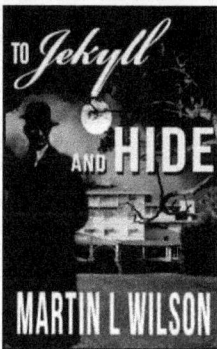

THE FIELD OF JUSTICE
MOONSHINE AND MURDER IN NORTH GEORGIA
WILLIAM A. THOMAS, JR.

James Everett Kibler
Tiller

A FATAL MERCY
The Man Who Lost The Civil War
A Novel By THOMAS MOORE

RANDALL IVEY
THE GIFT OF GAB

MAXCY GREGG'S SPORTING JOURNALS 1842-1858
SUZANNE PARFITT JOHNSON, EDITOR
FOREWORD BY JAMES EVERETT KIBLER, JR.

An Aesthetic Education and Other Stories

CHAINED TREE, CHAINED OWLS
POEMS
CATHARINE SAVAGE BROSMAN

Carolina Twilight
KAREN STOKES

SPLINTERED
Frandi Perry

TO Jekyll AND HIDE
MARTIN L WILSON

RUNAWAY HALEY
An Imagined Family Saga
2021 WINNER
WILLIAM A. THOMAS JR.

THE IMMORTALS
Karen Stokes

GREEN ALTAR BOOKS
SHOTWELL PUBLISHING

GA

Green Altar (Literary Imprint)

CATHARINE SAVAGE BROSMAN
*An Aesthetic Education
and Other Stories (2nd Ed)*

Chained Tree, Chained Owls: Poems

Aerosols and Other Poems

Partial Memoirs

RANDALL IVEY
*A New England Romance:
And Other Southern Stories*

The Gift of Gab

SUZANNE JOHNSON
Maxcy Gregg's Sporting Journals 1842-1858

JAMES E. KIBLER, JR.
Tiller : Claybank County Series, Vol. 4

The Gentler Gamester

*In the Deep Heart's Core: Poems of Tribute and
Remembrance (forthcoming)*

THOMAS MOORE
*A Fatal Mercy:
The Man Who Lost The Civil War*

PERRIN LOVETT
The Substitute, Tom Ironsides 1

KAREN STOKES
Belles

Carolina Twilight

Honor in the Dust

The Immortals

The Soldier's Ghost: A Tale of Charleston

WILLIAM THOMAS
*Runaway Haley:
An Imagined Family Saga*

*The Field of Justice: Moonshine
and Murder in North Georgia*

CLYDE N. WILSON
*Southern Poets and Poems, 1606 -1860:
The Land They Loved, Volume 1*

*Confederate Poets and Poems, Vol 1
The Land They Loved, Volume II*

Gold-Bug
(Mystery & Suspense Imprint)

BRANDI PERRY
Splintered: A New Orleans Tale

MARTIN WILSON
To Jekyll and Hide

THE SOUTH'S FINEST CONTEMPORARY AUTHORS.

Shotwell Publishing is proud to be called home by many of today's most respected Southern scholars and literary greats.

JEFFERY ADDICOTT
Union Terror: Debunking the False Justifications for Union Terror

Trampling Union Terror: Riders of the Second Alabama Cavalry

MARK ATKINS
Women in Combat: Feminism Goes to War

JOYCE BENNETT
Maryland, My Maryland: The Cultural Cleansing of a Small Southern State

GARRY BOWERS
Slavery and The Civil War: What Your History Teacher Didn't Tell You

Dixie Days: Reminiscences Of a Southern Boyhood

JERRY BREWER
Dismantling the Republic

ANDREW P. CALHOUN
My Own Darling Wife: Letters From A Confederate Volunteer

JOHN CHODES
Segregation: Federal Policy or Racism?

Washington's KKK: The Union League During Southern Reconstruction

WALTER BRIAN CISCO
War Crimes Against Southern Civilians

DAVID T. CRUM
Stonewall Jackson: Saved by Providence

JOHN DEVANNY
Continuities: The South in a Time of Revolution

Lincoln's Continuing Revolution: Essays of M.E. Bradford and Thomas H. Landess

JOSHUA DOGGRELL
Doxed: The Political Lynching of a Southern Cop

JAMES C. EDWARDS
What Really Happened?: Quantrill's Raid On Lawrence, Kansas

TED EHMANN
Boom & Bust In Bone Valley: Florida's Phosphate Mining History 1886-2021

JOHN AVERY EMISON
The Deep State Assassination of Martin Luther King Jr.

DON GORDON
Snowball's Chance: My Kidneys Failed, My Wife Left Me & My Dog Died...

JOHN R. GRAHAM
Constitutional History of Secession

PAUL C. GRAHAM
Confederaphobia

When The Yankees Come: Former Carolina Slaves Remember

Nonsense on Stilts: The Gettysburg Address & Lincoln's Imaginary Nation

JOE D. HAINES
The Diary of Col. John Henry Stover Funk of the Stonewall Brigade, 1861-1862

KAREN STOKES
A Legion Of Devils: Sherman In South Carolina

*The Burning of Columbia, S.C.: A Review
of Northern Assertions and Southern Facts*

Carolina Love Letters

*Fortunes of War:
The Adventures of a German Confederate*

*A Confederate in Paris:
Letters of A. Dudley Mann 1867-1879*

JOSEPH R. STROMBERG
*Southern Story and Song:
Country Music in the 20th Century*

JACK TROTTER
Last Train to Dixie

JOHN THEURSAM
Key West's Civil War

H.V. TRAYWICK, JR.
*Along The Shadow Line:
A Road Trip through History and Memory
on the Old Confederate Border*

LESLIE TUCKER
*Old Times There Should Not Be Forgotten:
Cultural Genocide In Dixie*

JOHN VINSON
Southerner Take Your Stand!

MARK R. WINCHELL
*Confessions of a Copperhead:
Culture and Politics in the Modern South*

CLYDE N. WILSON
Calhoun: A Statesman for the 21st Century

*Lies My Teacher Told Me: The True History
of the War For Southern Independence*

The Yankee Problem: An American Dilemma

*Annals Of The Stupid Party:
Republicans Before Trump*

*Nullification:
Reclaiming The Consent of the Governed*

The Old South: 50 Essential Books

The War Between The States: 60 Essential Books

*Reconstruction and the New South, 1865-1913:
50 Essential Books*

*The South 20th Century And Beyond:
50 Essential Books*

*Southern Poets and Poems, 1606-1860:
The Land They Loved, Volume 1*

*Confederate Poets and Poems, Vol 1
The Land They Loved, Volume II*

Looking For Mr. Jefferson

African American Slavery in Historical Perspective

JOE WOLVERTON
*What Degree Of Madness?: Madison's Method
To Make American States Again*

WALTER KIRK WOOD
*Beyond Slavery: The Northern Romantic
Nationalist Origins of America's Civil War*

SHOTWELL
COLUMBIA · SO. CAR.
EST. 2015
PUBLISHING

SHOTWELLPUBLISHING.COM

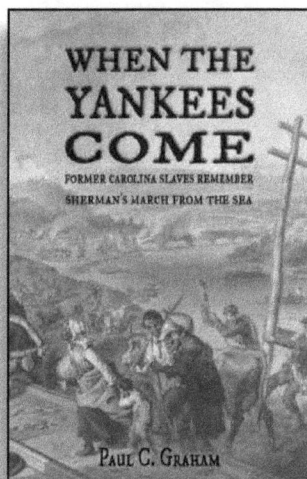

Free Book Offer

DON'T GET LEFT OUT, Y'ALL.

Sign-up and be the first to know about new releases, sales, and other goodies
—plus we'll send you TWO FREE EBOOKS!

Lies My Teacher Told Me:
The True History of the War for
Southern Independence
by Dr. Clyde N. Wilson

&

When The Yankees Come
Former Carolina Slaves Remember
Sherman's March From the Sea
by Paul C. Graham

FreeLiesBook.com

Southern Books. No Apologies.

We love the South — its history,
traditions, and culture — and are proud
of our inheritance as Southerners.
Our books are a reflection of this love.

www.ingramcontent.com/pod-product-compliance
Lightning Source LLC
Chambersburg PA
CBHW072144090426
42739CB00013B/3280